¡Criaturas diminutas!/Bugs, Bugs, Bugs!

Arañas/Spiders

por/by Margaret Hall

Traducción/Translation: Dr. Martín Luis Guzmán Ferrer
Editor Consultor/Consulting Editor: Dra. Gail Saunders-Smith

Consultor/Consultant: Gary A. Dunn, MS, Director of Education
Young Entomologists' Society Inc.
Lansing, Michigan

Capstone
press®

Mankato, Minnesota

Pebble Plus is published by Capstone Press,
151 Good Counsel Drive, P.O. Box 669, Mankato, Minnesota 56002.
www.capstonepress.com

122009
005643R

Library of Congress Cataloging-in-Publication Data
Hall, Margaret, 1947–
    [Spiders. Spanish & English]
    Arañas = Spiders/de/by Margaret Hall.
    p. cm.—(Pebble plus. ¡Criaturas diminutas!/Bugs, bugs, bugs!)
    Includes index.
    ISBN-13: 978-0-7368-6677-4 (hardcover)
    ISBN-10: 0-7368-6677-9 (hardcover)
    1. Spiders—Juvenile literature. I. Title: Spiders. II. Title. III. Pebble plus. ¡Criaturas diminutas!
(Spanish & English)
    QL458.4.H34 2007
    595.44—dc22   2005037466

Summary: Simple text and photographs describe the physical characteristics and habits of spiders—in both
    English and Spanish.

Editorial Credits
Sarah L. Schuette, editor; Katy Kudela, bilingual editor; Eida del Risco, Spanish copy editor; Linda Clavel,
    set designer; Kelly Garvin, photo researcher; Karen Hieb, product planning editor

Photo Credits
Ann & Rob Simpson, 7
Bill Johnson, 4–5
Bruce Coleman Inc./David Lushewitz, 16–17; Gary Meszaros, 10–11; Michael Fogen, 15
David Liebman, 20–21
DigitalVision/Gerry Ellis & Michael Durham, 1
Pete Carmichael, cover, 8–9, 12–13, 19

Note to Parents and Teachers

The ¡Criaturas diminutas!/Bugs, Bugs, Bugs! set supports national science standards related to the diversity of life and heredity. This book describes spiders in both English and Spanish. The images support early readers in understanding the text. The repetition of words and phrases helps early readers learn new words. This book also introduces early readers to subject-specific vocabulary words, which are defined in the Glossary section. Early readers may need assistance to read some words and to use the Table of Contents, Glossary, Internet Sites, and Index sections of the book.

Table of Contents

Tabla de contenidos

Spiders

What are spiders?

Spiders are arachnids.

Las arañas

¿Qué son las arañas?

Las arañas son arácnidos.

4

How Spiders Look

Many spiders are black,
brown, or gray. Some
spiders have furry bodies.

Cómo son las arañas

Muchas arañas son negras,
marrones o grises. Algunas
arañas tienen el cuerpo peludo.

Some spiders are about
the size of a fist. Other
spiders are about the size
of a dime.

Algunas arañas son casi
del tamaño de un puño.
Otras arañas pueden ser
del tamaño de una monedita.

Spiders have eight legs.
They feel sounds with
their legs. Spiders do not
have ears.

Las arañas tienen ocho patas.
Con sus patas sienten los sonidos.
Las arañas no tienen oídos.

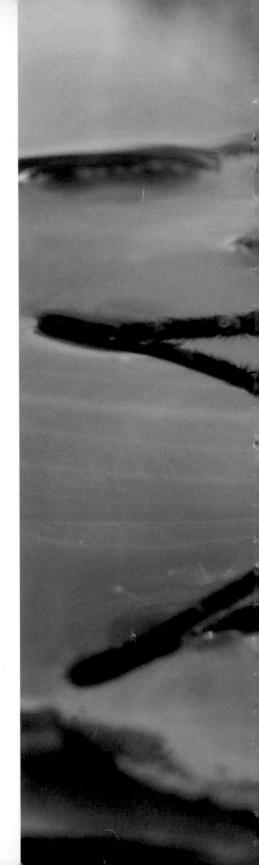

Spiders have many eyes.
Most spiders have
eight eyes.

Las arañas tienen muchos
ojos. La mayoría de
las arañas tiene ocho ojos.

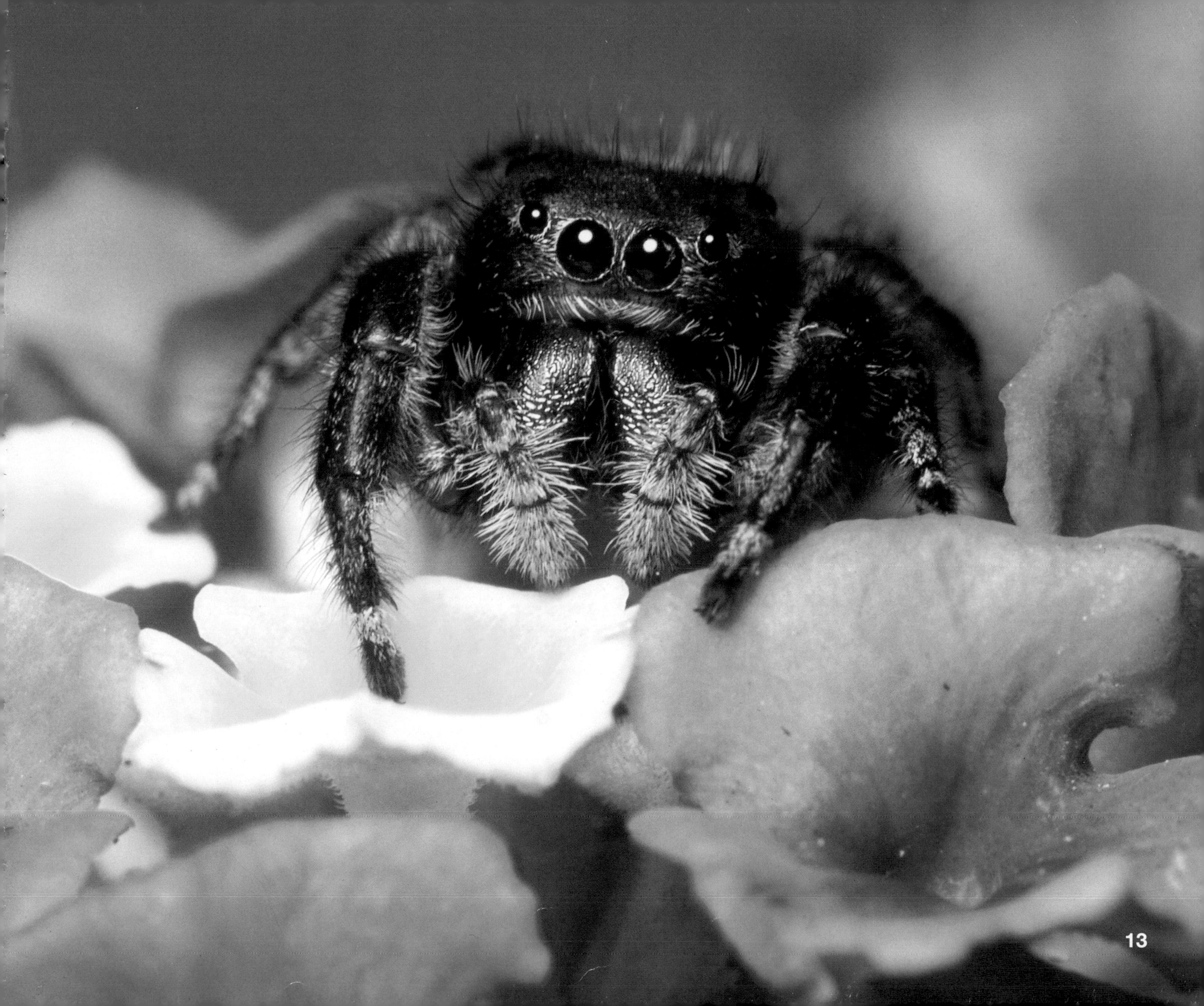

Spiders have two fangs.

The fangs are hollow.

Las arañas tienen dos colmillos.

Sus colmillos son huecos.

15

What Spiders Do

Some spiders spin webs.
They eat food that gets
stuck in the webs.

Qué hacen las arañas

Algunas arañas tejen
telarañas. Se comen
la comida que se queda
pegada en sus telarañas.

16

Some spiders jump on their
food. They eat insects.

Algunas arañas se
lanzan sobre su comida.
Las arañas comen insectos.

Some spiders go fishing.

They catch and eat fish.

Algunas arañas se van de pesca.

Atrapan peces y se los comen.

Glossary

arachnid—a small animal with eight legs, two body sections, and no wings or antennas; spiders, scorpions, mites, and ticks are arachnids.

fang—a long, hollow tooth; a poison called venom flows through fangs.

insect—a small animal with a hard outer shell, six legs, three body sections, and two antennas; most insects have wings.

web—a fine net of silky threads

Glosario

el arácnido—animal pequeño de ocho patas,
cuerpo de dos secciones, sin alas ni antenas;
la araña, el alacrán, el arador de las sarna y la
garrapata son arácnidos.

el colmillo—diente alargado y hueco; un veneno
llamado ponzoña sale a través de los colmillos.

el insecto—animal pequeño con un caparazón
duro, seis patas, cuerpo de tres secciones y
dos antenas; la mayoría de los insectos
tiene alas.

la telaraña—red fina de hilos sedosos

Internet Sites

FactHound offers a safe, fun way to find Internet sites related to this book. All of the sites on FactHound have been researched by our staff.

Here's how:

1. Visit *www.facthound.com*

2. Choose your grade level.

3. Type in this book ID **0736866779** for age-appropriate sites. You may also browse subjects by clicking on letters, or by clicking on pictures and words.

4. Click on the **Fetch It** button.

FactHound will fetch the best sites for you!

Sitios de Internet

FactHound proporciona una manera divertida y segura de encontrar sitios de Internet relacionados con este libro. Nuestro personal ha investigado todos los sitios de FactHound. Es posible que los sitios no estén en español.

Se hace así:

1. Visita *www.facthound.com*

2. Elige tu grado escolar.

3. Introduce este código especial **0736866779** para ver sitios apropiados según tu edad, o usa una palabra relacionada con este libro para hacer una búsqueda general.

4. Haz clic en el botón **Fetch It**.

¡FactHound buscará los mejores sitios para ti!